The Girl

This Is My Testimony

Dr. Bella Johnson

DEDICATION

This Book is dedicated to my kids Journey, Jo'Syah, and Jade. For so long mommy never knew who she was until now! I apologize publicly for all the hell I put you all through. It wasn't intentional, but my careless decisions did affect you all in some type of way that I never realized. Although mommy never let you guys see me sweat, it was a time that I tried to give up. God wouldn't let me so remember mommy's story so you can be better and wont go through what I went through. I love y'all!

Y'all SuperHero,

Mommy

Fun Facts About My Book Cover

The Giraffe

My Favorite animal is a giraffe, because of their long lashes and they stand tall in their environment. They spend most of their time standing up. It reminds me to stand no matter what the circumstances are and look good while doing it.

The Dandelion

The Dandelion on the cover represents a dandelion. Lol
I think of myself as such, because I flow as the wind blows. At times, I feel like I'm being blown into many directions.

The Flower

I love flowers, because it reminds me of God's perfection. It starts off as a seed then blooms into something so beautiful. Reminds me of myself. Something so small blooming so big and beautiful (I'm not even talking about looks). I stop in my tracks and take time to smell them no matter where I am. They take my breath away just like giraffes.

The Torn Picture

Simple! The enemy ripped me into pieces, but God put me back together again!

CONTENTS

ACKNOWLEDGMENTS

*Disclaimer: I didn't want an editor. I wanted to write how I talk. I didn't need anyone twisting my words to make them sound fancy. That's not me so I hope that you find it humorous and enjoy my slang, run on sentences, and possible misspelled words.

Now, I would like to thank you for using your hard earned money to buy a book about a young woman who's not famous, but is just someone giving her life testimony in hopes that someone can use this and overcome whatever it is that they're facing! Thanks from the bottom of my heart.

-Dr. Bella J

1: THE LITTLE MISSIONARY

I remember sitting in church with my sister and grandmother wondering where is this God that they were preaching about. I would hear about how God gave his only begotten son, thinking wow I hope my mom don't give me up. I watched and giggled as they ran around the church shouting and proclaiming to cast out demons. I never understood. After church, my sister and I would go home and re-enact everything that we seen in church. She use to anoint my head with spit to cast out my demons and I would catch the "Holy Ghost" and started shouting. My Grandma, which was a pastor, would catch us and instantly started calling me Shirley Caesar. We overheard her telling her Bishop about how we would come home doing everything that we had seen so he started calling us the little missionaries.

I was young so I didn't know what that meant, but I knew it had something to do with that long boring church service. Remind you that we stayed in church seemed like everyday, Monday-Sunday so I knew how service would go, what they was going to say, and who was going to fall out. I was programmed and tired of whoever God was and his son. Then here comes summer and we began vacation bible school, by this time I could teach the class with everything I had learned in church. Not understanding why my grandmother kept me in church, until that same God that I was tired of had to reach way down and pull me up out of my mess later on in life.

My mother was busy working trying to provide for me and I didn't know who my father was so my grandmother & grandfather raised me. They protected me from the world as long as they could. I soon began to become curious about what the world had to offer.

2: LIL DANGEROUS

My cousins was older than me and had more freedom so I wanted to hang with them at Madear house to get a break from this church life. I began to try alcohol and joined a gang. I was a tom boy with a mouth full of gold teeth. I admired my boy cousins so much. They were the face of Paterson Court and nobody didn't want to go to war with them Turner boys. They taught me some things, but most importantly get them before they get you. My cousin, Mike, made me fight everyday until I won. I had to fight the little girl in the projects that never lost a fight. I was terrified lol. That girl whooped me bad so my cousin made me fight his little brother to help me win next time. The next day came and I seen the lil Mike Tyson, the little girl that whooped me yesterday, walking to the candy lady. I yelled "rematch".

I was still scared, but I learned some new moves and to keep my head up while fighting. Safe to say I didn't lose that time. You couldn't tell me nothing now. We was a fighting family. My cousin then gave me the name "Lil Dangerous". I felt like I made it and now I wanted to fight anybody that I seen walking.

True story: My sister tricked me at the movies like a girl rolled her eyes at her and had me chasing the girl in the parking lot to beat her up. The girl was yelling "I didn't do anything..I promise." Yes, I beat that girl up for no reason.

Hold on y'all! Im saved now.. let me make this right.

Dear Girl that I beat up for no reason & everybody else that I put my hands on or shot at,

If you're reading this..I'm sorry. I didn't know any better. Please forgive me!

Back to the story..

My grandmother was so disappointed when she found out I went astray, in her words. She said she wash her hands with me, because she was tired. That was just what I needed to hear. Now I can go home and stay with my mom.

3: LIL HALF PINT

I knew my mom worked a lot so we could do whatever we wanted to do at night. I became interested in boys and my sister and I turned our house into a club. We had that house jumping. We use to drink all of my mom liquor and fill it back up with water like she wouldn't notice. We was known for throwing the best house parties. We went from the little missionaries to the lil city girls now! Lol we was turnt and out there dragging my grandma image through the mud. My mom was known as Half-Pint, but she was dangerous on that dance floor. We swore nobody could beat us in dancing. Once my cousin Dre tell me to stir them grits (my famous dance move) it was on and popping! I would hit a split, walk the dog, stack on top of each other, then hit the cry baby and everybody would go crazy.

Now I look back, I was a baby exotic dancer! My mama made me compete in the projects every gathering the hood had. My mama use to bring the city out and everybody would stand there watching me pop and shake it. I just knew my cousin's friends wanted me. I bet they was like "Guh sit yo lil fast self down" lol I was attracted to older guys so I started dating a 16 year old when I was 12. He lived in the country, but he use to come up and see me at night. Although, I was being fast..I was still a virgin. One night he came and we sat in his van talking about sex and he was so uneasy. He didn't want to be the one to take my virginity. He said he didn't want to hurt me. My peers had lost their virginity so I was curious. We ended up having sex and I almost fainted. That was the worst pain ever. I use to help my aunt out with my lil cousin while she worked long hours so I became a mother before I became a mother. It made me grow up so quick & I wasn't interested in sex anymore. I found myself questioning my peers like why y'all like that. One of them told me that's what make them love you & just like an idiot I believed it. I just knew I would end up gay, because I didn't want to lay down ever again with a boy.

4:LAGB
(LIL A** GANG BANGER)

My peers and I was very close. We formed a gang called "L.A.G.B," Lil A** Gang Bangers. It was full of young girls and I was one of the ring leaders. We gave ourselves tattoos with erasers so we could be official. Yes, scrubbed our skin off. The oldest in the group was from Lowndes County (45) so she introduced us to the country life. I use to have so much fun at her house that when my mom use to make me come home, I would act a fool. I fell in love with dolphins so my precious mother took her hard earned money and decorated my room in dolphins. I had a lot of glass dolphin sculptures and I would throw everything off my dresser and just scream to the top of my lungs. "I hate you mom"..just kidding.

I wouldn't be writing this book if I said that back then lol. I would throw everything around though. One day I ran away to the country. She said I had 10 mins to get back home, but I was like how in the world can I get back home in that short amount of time. By the time I got home she killed me. As she would say " Don't make me stop your breathing for 25 secs." She was a correction officer at the women's prison and learned those lil moves, trying to come home and do them on me. I was the problem child for sure. My oldest sister and lil brother use to look at me like I was a possessed demon. I was the one who would challenge my mama in a fight even though I knew she would put me to sleep every time. We began to have a love hate relationship, because she felt I just wanted to see her hurt behind me. I would see her crying and in my lil demonic head I would say "Keep on faking imma give you some to cry about!" I wanted to knock her head off for beating me that bad. I had belt marks all over me. Those moves my cousin, Mike, taught me..didn't work on mama.

One day, I said I know how to make her hurt. Our cellphone was turned off and I snuck in her wallet and paid our phone bill. She found out and tried to kill me again. That was our rent money. I said " Well you gotta start paying your bills."

5: BOO-BOO

My nickname growing up was "BooBoo" and if it was some drama better believe "BooBoo" had something to do with it.

It was now time for me to go to high school. I was still thugging, but I had calmed down a lot. I wasn't fighting as much just when I had to. I had met my high school sweetheart and I didn't care to be that tom boy "BooBoo" anymore. I wanted to tap into my girly side to impress him. I use to wear heels everyday to school. Like what was I thinking lol. I remember falling out in those very heels and they had to rush me to the hospital. I woke up in the hospital to my mom and peers surrounding me. My appendix had ruptured and nearly killed me. That scared me and I remembered that man my grandmother cried and prayed to so I began to say "Jesus help me". I was in so much pain. I was young and didn't understand why this was happening to me. That incident slowed me down a lot.

When I returned to school I was showered with so much love. I had no interest in being messy nor fighting, but somehow the enemy tried to get me while I was still healing. A girl was walking down the hallway and bumped me and I yelled "you need to watch where you going bald headed trick" and she said simply " I got you". Not knowing what she got, but she tried to get my high school sweetheart.

Everybody knew I didn't play about that boy, periodt. I avoided her until I healed up so she picked with me for weeks. I bit my tongue, because I knew if she hit me in my stomach, where my wounds were then somebody was going to die.

The day finally came where we was face to face in the gym. It had been so long that I forgot about her, but she didn't forget about me. As I was walking away, she yelled "square up BooBoo". I kept walking and she pushed me. At that moment I tried to kill whatever was in my way to get to her. I ended up fighting the principal and the assistant principal. I seen red and blanked out. When I came back down to earth I was locked up in the Juvenile Detention Facility.

I asked was the other girl that I was fighting there and they said no. Only to find out that I broke the assistant principal nose so I was facing an assault charge. I sat in my bunk and cried. I laid there talking to that man, Jesus, that my grandmother taught me about.

I ended up getting released on house arrest and probation after a week, but I couldn't return to school.

I found myself sitting there sad blaming my mom for me not having a father in my life to help me not get in trouble. I blamed everybody, but myself.

Just when I thought things couldn't get worst...my granddaddy died. The only man that I felt loved me. He was my favorite person. He took a piece of me when he left. It was that moment that I wrote him a poem and told him that I would make him proud.

I left LAGB behind and went to the local college to get my GED. I knew that I would pass it on my first try and off to college I went.

As I mentioned before, I grew up in Paterson Court and I remember hearing the band playing at Alabama State University, which was across the street. I said I want to go to that college when I grow up so once I had the opportunity..I took it.

I started ASU in the fall of 2008. I enrolled for Biology Pre-Med and hated it so I eventually switched to forensic science. While on campus, I met a guy that was a club promoter. He was so calm and taught me how to be calm. He introduced me to the infamous clubs "The Rose & Frontstreet." I wanted to be different. The girls I was hanging around on campus was bougie so I became bougie. People couldn't believe it. I wanted a new identity. During a spring break trip to Daytona, this guy said your mom should have name you "Bella," because you're so beautiful. That was the day I held a funeral for "BooBoo' and celebrated the birth of "Bella".

I left my past behind me and went to further my education as "Bella". I wasn't as bougie as I thought.

<u>True story: One day we went to the club and security called me out of my name, because I wouldn't give him no play and I maced him and drove off. I didn't go to that club for a while. I called myself going to another club and he was in there. I told the gang that we was going to have to go ahead and beat him up, but I guess he was now scared of me..he walked up to me, hugged me, and apologized lol.</u>

Dear Security Man that I maced that night in the parking lot,

if you're reading this book…. I'm sorry.

Back to the story.. I guess I was a man magnet because they were coming my way. Yes, I was choosing. Listen it was raining men!! My calm boyfriend got tired of my doggish ways and left me. I was devastated when he followed me to his cousin house and as I was sitting in the car, he knocked on the window. Hold on y'all! I didn't know that was that man cousin give me some grace. He moved on and I ended up beating up his girlfriend just because.

My sadness didn't last long. I Met a military guy/cop and knew I wasn't ready to settle down, but I did it anyway and 6 months later I ran away from the commitment. That was the start of my awful commitment cycle. My mother always told me that if I wasn't happy then leave so that stuck with me.

My Mama Favorite Toxic Quotes

- LIFE IS TOO SHORT NOT TO BE HAPPY!
- WHAT 1 MAN WONT DO, THE OTHER WILL!
- I CAN DO BAD BY MYSELF!

-HALF PINT

I never knew that listening to mama would damage me in the end. I thought mama was always right.

*We must forgive our parents for not teaching us the right way, because they didn't know. Give them grace just as Christ gave us!"

7: SHIRLEY CAESAR

One day, my sister called me and told me that she wanted me to meet a lady that can really preach and prophesy. She told me that the lady was an Apostle. I'm like what is that? She explained and I eventually went to visit the church. After going a couple of times, I joined the church and I started to form a relationship with that man I once didn't fully know. I began to know him for myself and began to serve him.

It was an awesome experience and I began to crave more of Jesus. I'll never forget when I finally caught the holy ghost. I couldn't control myself I caught out running like the women in church use to when I was little. I began to cry out and speak in tongues. I was scared and didn't realize what had happened. When it was over the Apostle said, "You caught the Holy Ghost". I couldn't wait to tell my grandma what had happened.

8:NURS B

Apostle prophesied to me that I would preach the word and I looked at her like baby you got the wrong one. I told my grandma after church and she agreed and said " You were called in your mothers womb! You will preach the word before I leave this earth." I thought both of them were crazy. I began to start my walk with christ. I became conflicted with trying to stay focus and going out to party. I ended up meeting a guy while headed to a college party. It was a road block and he approached my car. I began to flirt and spit that game to him so we had to exchange numbers. A year later I was pregnant & we settled down. I always thought I couldn't get pregnant. Crazy right? I was so sick with my daughter that I missed a whole semester of school.

I had no choice, but to dropped out of ASU and go to nursing school. I couldn't continue walking that campus with my big belly. My oldest daughter was born and I thought that this is it! This is my forever. Nope!, things wasn't going my way so of course my mama is always right so it was time to go. I started noticing the cycles and I slowly lost interest in Jesus. It was like my whole family was struggling and we couldn't help each other. My daughter and I went from house to house. The last house we went to the bed bugs tore us up. Our skin was on fire lol. I refused to go back over there.

One night it was raining and my baby fell asleep in the car so we just slept in the car. It was late I just cried. I felt like my life was over. I revealed to my guy friend, who was married, what was going on & he bought us a hotel room that next night. Soon my classmate let me stay at her house for a while then my grandma got back on her feet and we went to live with her. This was the motivation that I needed. I began to work at the local hospital at night so I could finish up my nursing degree. I didn't have time for my daughter and it hurt me when my grandma would mention it.

Times got hard and I found myself doing anything for money. I turned to pimping women and selling drugs. BRICKS! ALL WHITE BRICKS…you know the rest. I started to hear clearly and consistently from God at this point. God would always convict me and I would tell him, " Im going to stop soon."

One day headed to my stop, a guy hit the back of my car and I ran off the road. He jumped out and tried to rob me. It didn't go as planned, but that was the wake up I needed and I stopped it all.

Nursing school took a little longer to complete due to me not making that fast money anymore and me not being in class, but I made it out after I delivered my son. Yes, I couldn't stay single long. Guess what? I settled down again thinking ok I have a career things will be better.

Well, I still didn't know who I was and the guy was an awesome person. He kept me in church every Sunday. We would worship together and I learned that I loved to worship. It was just damaged me. I missed Rosa Parks! Ok ok lol just kidding. I searched for my granddaddy love in these men and it wasn't adding up to what I needed.

9: BELLA B

I told myself you're not getting with nobody else son hurting them so I took a break from dating. Hold on y'all…

Dear Men That I dogged out and broke y'all hearts, I'm sorry..it wasn't intentional. I had some underlying mental health issues that I wasn't aware of. Please forgive me, because I know y'all bought this book to see if your name was in here lol. Nope, wont sue me for my lil proceeds.

Cousins y'all know when folks think you made it, they will try to do anything to get some fame. Get back Satans!

Back to the story..

I began to focus on my kids. I had friends, but I didn't try to commit because I knew I couldn't. I remember thinking what is wrong with me why cant I just be with one person. I heard a still voice that said " Im all that you need, love me first". Im a nut so I told God " you cant keep me warm at night" lol.

Years of being a player went by and I was minding my business and here comes this man asking to spoil me. I'm not going to turn that down. We dated and it came with so many demons that I had to fight. I learned how to fight in the spiritual realm, but at times I had to fight physically. He moved me all over the state to protect me from drama, but that didn't help. One of his mistress resurrected "BooBoo" from the dead.

I found myself in and out of jail with criminal charges. I had to go to court referral programs so now my nursing license was in jeopardy. At that moment I knew I had to escape the drama. Years went by and we decided to make it work. One day I was headed home in the car with my sister and got into a car wreck. I was ok at the scene, but then once I got to the hospital I couldn't move my right side. I was temporarily paralyzed from the right shoulder down to my foot. I had to learn how to walk again. I was telling my arm to move, but it wouldn't. I called my husband at the time and told him and he never showed up to the hospital. I had a talk with God and told him that I was tired and to deliver me from this man.

It's like I couldn't leave him despite all the pain he was causing me. I found out I was pregnant and it was the loneliest pregnancy ever. They admitted me into the hospital for some pregnancy complications and that's when I began to write this book, but it started as "The Hatching," because I knew God was developing me and soon it would be time to hatch and go forth.

My grandmother felt my pain and finally told me who my father was. My mom wouldn't tell me, because they had a bad deal back in the day and my dad was married. I looked his name up on facebook and dropped the phone. I resembled this man and his daughter was my twin. I inboxed him and a month later I got a response. God knew I needed someone so he sent my biological father to me. We bonded and it was like I knew him my whole life. He gave me what I was missing from my grand father. I began to start feeling healed each day I was around him.

One night, I went to bed in the hospital and the doctor woke me up saying that my baby vitals was decreasing and that I was going to have an emergency c-section. My husband was out somewhere drunk so I begged him to get to the hospital quick. He came and my baby girl was born.

I was relieved because she was here healthy but also it was pay back time. Yes, I was petty. Well, two weeks later he got arrested for some unheard of charges and I began to feel free. I missed him and wanted him with his daughter, but I also remembered that he hurt me and abandoned me.

It was hard being away from him trying to hold everything down, but I made it work. I started to enjoy my life, take trips, just live.

I moved to Dallas to get a new start. Thinking he's going off to prison for some years, they decided to let him do community corrections. He told me that I needed to get back to Alabama because he would need a physical address in Bama so he could come home. I moved back to save my marriage and got an apartment.

10: THE RETURN OF BOOBOO

My relationship with God was shaky so I didn't consult with God about nothing. I just did it. I left my fully furnished home in Texas all because I wanted my daughter to know her dad. He told me that they put him in a halfway house and he would get passes to come see us.

That went on for a month and my baby started to not want him to leave. As he left, I seen a car block him in and a woman started cursing at him. I got curious. I called his phone and no answer so the next day my mom told me that she seen him in the nail salon with a lady and her child. I said naw ma that cant be him…he used up all his visitation passes. I was on alert now. He came over that night and I said let me use the car to go to the store. He lied and said it was his homeboy car. I went through the car and behold this man had been out of jail and living with a woman. I got the address and all the evidence I needed to confront him.

I went back to the apartment and a phone dinged from under the seat. It was the mistress. She told him that maybe I found out and that he should just stay with me because she didn't want to be in the drama. Now, this one done resurrected BooBoo. Just when I thought I changed, here comes the bomb. I got him in the car and the rest was history. He stayed that night and I stayed up just thinking how this man played me. Lied about having a homeboy named "Jake" and all. I remember riding way to Birmingham to pass by the facility to see if I would see him in the yard. He texted me that he was in class so I never seen him.

How you play the player! Lol I always filed for a divorce to piss him off ,but this time I was serious. He brung me back to Alabama to do me like this. Then you cheating on me with a scarecrow...I crashed out. Literally, I woke up in a helicopter over looking the city. I met that man that I've been longing to meet. Yes, Jesus. He stood over me with my grandfather. Blood was everywhere.

11:MINISTER B

I heard in background chatter saying "if she make it through this then that will be a miracle."

Not knowing what was happening I said "granddaddy I cant keep going through this! Come get me! Jesus please take me!"

Jesus replied " Your work isn't done, back you go!"

I woke up on a surgical table with two gunshot wounds to my head. My head was shaved and I went back out. The next time I woke up, I got up to use the restroom and I looked in the mirror and my head was wrapped like a mummy. I couldn't believe that I had been shot and still alive. The doctor said if you can survive a 9mm to the head going in and coming out with no damage to your skull then you need to write a book. So here we are!

They ended up sending me to the psych ward. I wasn't afraid I just wanted some rest. I was over stimulated and was just ready to get all of this over. I missed my kids so my sister would bring them to the window and I would sit there all day hoping they would ride by.

My father and mom came to visit me and I could see the hurt in their eyes looking at me with a shaved head. While in there I began to worship God with the other patients. I got special treatment because I was a nurse, but I wanted them to treat me just as the others. It was at that moment I began to tell the others of how God saved my life and gave me another chance.

The psychiatrist began to tell me the story of what happened, because I didn't remember & still don't know all of the details. I was shocked. I was found inside of my truck shot and my truck was inside the mistress house. He said you went out with a bang literally. I got discharged after 14 days and it was time to turn myself in. We payed my bond before I turned myself in so all I had to do was sign in and take a photo then I was free to go until court.

A couple of days later my soon to be ex-husband filed for emergency custody of my daughter. I lost my daughter and It took everything in me to not bury him and the mistress.

My baby cried as they pulled her away from me to go stay with this woman she didn't know and her dad whom she just got to know. I was empty without my child. DHR got involved and I had to have regular visits until they investigated. I remember my family being around me and comforting me. My father spent the night so I wouldn't be alone. I had cried so much..I was numb. I heard God say "Are you ready to love me & worship me yet?". I began to worship him instantly.

"You Can Run, But You Cant Hide!"

I began to become serious about my walk and Lord behold..My grandmother made me do a mock sermon. I began to grow my faith and get back in my word. I isolated myself from the world. I wrote a song called "surrender" and formed a ministry called "The Siscess Ministry". I took my focus off my situation and kept it on God.

Two weeks later, my daughter dad dropped my baby off and didn't come back. He said he couldn't do it and that he didn't want another woman raising his child. Of course, he tried to get his family back, but you couldn't pay me to get off track with God.

"Whatever you get in the world, You Must stay in the world to keep it!"

12: DR. B

Soon, I got ordained by my grandmother as a minister of the gospel and graduated from Theology school all in the midst of waiting for court. I preached my initial sermon and began to chase after GOD like never before. I guess what my grandmother & Apostle said was true.

It was now time for court and I prepared myself for the worst. I began to put my kids stuff in the storage because I knew I was going to prison. The lawyer told me to get ready to serve 2 years in the women's prison. I thought about my career and how I struggled to get through school just to hand it over to someone that wanted my life.

I was disappointed, but I still trusted God. I graduated from being a baby christian and was ready for battle. I started to bind up everything and speaking over my life. I walked out of court with a felony charge, but with 4 year probation. I didn't go to prison and I was relieved, however, I still had to face the board of nursing. I didn't dwell on the case. I left it in God's hands. A year later I was dismissed from my probation. My court date came for the Board and my lawyer said "Its not looking good.You might as well just give up your license for a year then reapply." At this point I started searching for other jobs just in case. My lawyer contacted me and said we don't have to go to court if you accept this offer. I knew it was over. MY GOD said naw! They granted me a 2 year probation sentence and I got to keep my license. I am now a Regional Director of Nursing all because my Father is BIGGER than my Felony. It doesn't even show up on my background check, but it's there.You cant tell me that God ain't Good!

After all of this I questioned God. I said God why did you take me through all of this? He said "You wanted to know what real love was so I had to show you. Despite how you ignored me, I still showed you grace and mercy. That's Love. In order for me to use you fully I needed to beef up your resume. Now that you have been through the test, you have a testimony. Now go tell everyone your testimony so they can see my goodness! Let them see me through you."

I just sat there speechless. I was embarrassed about my past, but here I am writing a book telling the world about what God has brung me through.

I pray that my testimony blesses you and let you know that it ain't over until God says it's over. During my rough journey I never lost the faith. It may have been small faith, but I had some. The bible says all you need is faith of a mustard seed & I had that.

While ministering I get asked how did you go through all of that and still kept a smile on your face? All I can say is by the grace of God. I never knew who I was. I never looked myself in the mirror and examined myself. I've always hid behind my career accomplishments.

One day I was running and I watched my shadow following me. I kept glancing back and wondered how people view me. It's not like I cared, but I wanted to know how people view that girl in the shadow. Would I be proud or embarrassed?, If I died today what would they say at my funeral?,or Would my funeral be packed?. All of these thoughts went through my head.

That day I began to ask God to create in me a clean heart and renew the right spirit within me. I started caring what others think. I started protecting my image. The things I use to say, I didn't say anymore, the places I use to go, I didn't go anymore! I wanted people to really see the God within me.

I wanted to leave an impact on my city. I was soon nominated as the 2024 woman of the year for the City of Montgomery.

I started being loud about God, going full force with my ministry, started accepting speaking engagements, being slow to anger, I literally let God take control of my life and decisions. My life isn't perfect, but its everything that I prayed for it to be. I can say that I'm full of joy no matter what comes my way. I refuse to let someone son or daughter steal my peace or joy. All of the glory belongs to God.

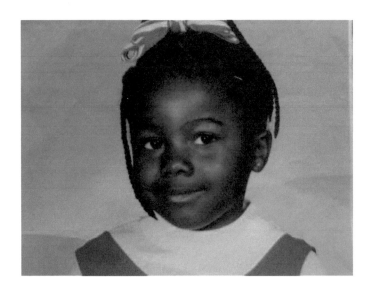

The Actual Girl in The Shadow!

I had so many identities, that I forgot about her. The young girl that didn't get a chance to just be a child and grow up. I had left her in the shadows to chase adulthood. I was grown before my time. I abandon this innocent soul when I should have been soaking in it. She was constantly following me around like what about me. If I knew then, what I know now....I would have brung that girl out of the shadow.

THIS IS MY TESTIMONY!

The Lil Missionaries

My Grandparents

My mama, sis, and me

The Girl In The Shadow

My aunt, sis, me, and Madear

Like mama like child! I was getting ready to stir them grits!

Mama,bro,sis,and me

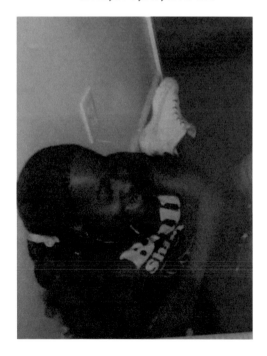

Me grilled out! Showing off my eraser
tattoo.

The little girl that made me a mother before I was a mother.

My cousin, Mike, First Day Out of Prison. Me in the red banging. Rip Queenie, Mike, and Lil-Bit

Front Street Days! Me in blue.

Rip Fuddie & Free The Real Ones!

Them Turners

Trina Kids

Linda Kids

(Rip Mike)

Bougalou Kids

(Rip Twan)

(Free King David)

The Girl In The Shadow

My Babies

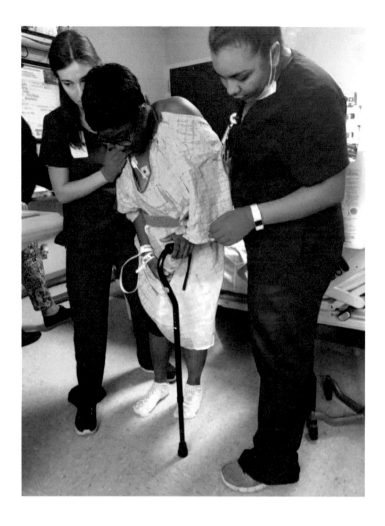

So when you see me praising God..now you will understand!

Just My Fav Mugshot..I had plenty more of them.

The Girl In The Shadow

I only suffer from occasional migraines & slight memory loss.

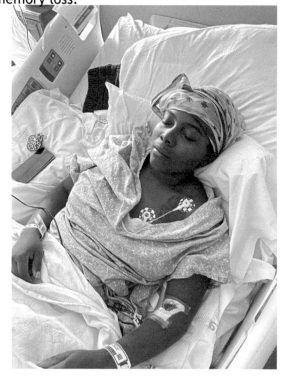

The Girl In The Shadow

The Lil Missionaries Became Missionaries!

The Girl In The Shadow

Giving Granny her flowers while she's alive!

Now Me & My sister have to share her with her other grandkids!

Mama you did the best that you could with raising us! We turned out pretty decent lol.
Sister-Teacher,Realtor,Minister, Entrepreneur
Mama-Social Worker & Entrepreneur
Me-Regional DON, Minster, Entrepreneur
Brother-Air Force,Social Work Manager &
Entrepreneur

The Girl In The Shadow

My Awesome Parents! Below is when me & Daddy first met.

The Girl In The Shadow

From GED to Doctorate!

Always give it your all and do your best!

You NEVER know who's watching!

In Loving Memory

Of

My Granddaddy

Madear

Mike (Lil Tiger)

Twan

Now can I minister to you for a sec..thanks

You cant tell God how to bless you & when to bless you! Sometimes you be expecting your blessing to come from Fed-Ex when he's sending it through USPS! Just because the box is beat up doesn't mean that you send it back.. the item on the inside is still intact the outside is just damaged.

For Christmas you wrap those gifts all nicely just for the kids to rip up the paper to see whats inside!

The inside is what matters the MOST! Check whats inside..its way more valuable!

A thief don't break into an empty house! It's something valuable inside of you that the enemy wants to steal from you! **The bible says "Be sober, be vigilant; because your adversary the devil, as a roaring lion, walketh about, seeking whom he may devour: 1 Peter 5:8.**

Whatever you are going through is just a test preparing you for your testimony! We all go through things. It's ok to fall, but don't stay down. Remember **Psalm 121: I will lift up mine eyes unto the hills, from whence cometh my help. My help cometh from the Lord, which made heaven and earth.**

Reflection

I now challenge you to take a moment and think back to when God brung you through a tough time. Write it down so you can come back to this book when you need a reminder of who God is.

_____

_____

_____

_____

_____

_____

_____

_____

_____

_____

_____

_____

_____

_____

_____

_____

_____

_____

_____

_____

_____

_____

_____

_____

_____

_____

And they overcame him by the blood of the Lamb, and by the word of their testimony; and they loved not their lives unto the death. Revelation 12:11

Do you know who you really are? Have you examined that girl or man in the shadow? List some things that you want God to change about you.

_____

_____

_____

_____

_____

_____

_____

_____

_____

_____

_____

Now Let's Pray!

Father God, I come to you as humble as I know how just to give you thanks for everything that you have did, done, and is going to do in my life. Now Father, I ask that you create in me a clean heart and renew the right spirit within me. I ask that you examine my list and remove anything that is not of you and even if its not on my list, I ask that you search my heart and do a clean sweep. I want to be made over Jesus! I surrender today! Please forgive me for all of my sins and help me to get it right. Let them see you within me Lord! Let me use my testimony to go forth and help others be delivered, in Jesus name! Amen!

Steps To Praying Dr. B Way

Believe it or not most people don't know how to pray! Its ok no one taught me. Remember, I mimicked what I heard in church as a little girl so let's go over how I do it.

1.Address Him/Adoration

"Father God", "Merciful Father", "Lord Jesus"

Acknowledge him/Give Praise

2. Give Thanks

"I just want to thank you for……"

Express your gratitude

3. Petition Him

Ask him for what you need, but make sure to pray for others

"Now I ask that you.."

4.Repent

Confess your sins and ask for forgiveness

"Father please forgive me for.."

5. Closing(Praise/Adoration Again)

Remind him of who he is & what his word say

"You are Alpha & Omega, The beginning & the end! You're the Lord of Lords, King of Kings!"

"In your word..You said…"

6. Seal it in his son name!

"In Jesus name!", "In the mighty name of Jesus!"

7.Confirmation/Agreement

"Amen"

I know you're probably wondering how in the world can I remind God of who he is if I don't know the word. Don't worry! I was the same way didn't know what his word truly was so I had to study. This was my way of studying.

These will help you learn about who Jesus is and some of his actions.

John

Mark

Matthew

Luke

These will talk about the first sin, law, and the Israelites

Genesis

Exodus

Leviticus

Numbers

Deuteronomy

You can go in order to the rest of the books now, this is how I learned & studied. Everyone is different and have their own ways of reading the Bible. I pray this helps!

Now that you have those important resources for your journey, let's talk about how are you mentally. For so long I have existed and never felt alive. I found help and it was the best thing that I could have done. Yes, you can rely on Jesus himself but he plant these gifts in others to help navigate you through life. Utilize them. When I started therapy I found out that I was battling things that I didn't know of. I found out why I couldn't stay committed in a relationship and all.

I challenge you to pray and reach out to a therapist. Find a mentor or an accountability partner. Guess what! You have me now to reach out to as well! Whether you need prayer, a mentor, advice, or at your breaking point..I'm Here.

Contact me via Email: thesiscessministry@gmail.com

Or Scan ->

<u>FUN FACT ABOUT DR. B</u>

I finally took the time to examine myself and find out what it truly was that I liked. I started to pay attention to what made me happy! I reflected on how my eyes would light up when I seen something green, a lime washed home, or when I seen a giraffe. Previous years I liked pink, dolphins, and red brick homes. It's amazing how when you learn yourself..you start to see things differently. We are so quick to become apart of the world and like what society like. Majority of every girl favorite color is pink. Well not mine. Dare to be different. God has set us apart. I challenge you to spend time with yourself & Jesus to learn who you really are. I have fallen in love with the woman that I am today. She's pretty dope! I finally have forgiven myself for my past mistakes!

I have NOW set that girl in the shadow free!

Made in the USA
Columbia, SC
04 March 2025

54697266R00044